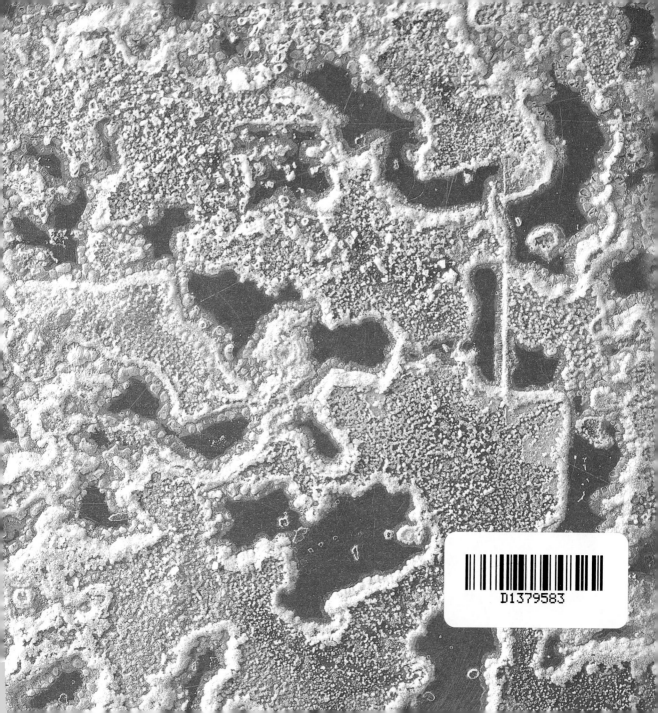

salt

salt

cooking with the
world's favorite
seasoning

Valerie Aikman-Smith
photography by Jonathan Gregson

RYLAND
PETERS
& SMALL

LONDON NEW YORK

Senior designer Megan Smith
Editors Delphine Lawrance & Clare Double
Production manager Hazel Kirkman
Art director Leslie Harrington
Publishing director Alison Starling

First published in 2009 by
Ryland Peters & Small
519 Broadway,
5th Floor
New York, NY 10012

www.rylandpeters.com

10 9 8 7 6 5 4 3 2 1

Text © Valerie
Aikman-Smith 2009
Design and photographs
© Ryland Peters & Small
2009

Printed and bound
in China

Library of Congress Cataloging-in-Publication Data
Salt : cooking with the world's favorite seasoning /
Valerie Aikman-Smith ; photography by
Jonathan Gregson. -- 1st U.S. ed.
    p. cm.
  ISBN 978-1-84597-912-6
  1. Condiments. 2. Salt. 3. Salting of food. I. Title.
  TX819.A1.A32 2009
  641.6--dc22
                                        2009012399

Contents

Introduction

Salt, heavenly salt—every cook's pantry is stocked with it. From everyday cooking salt to the pink rock salt of the Himalayas or the aromatic fleur de sel harvested in Guérande, France. There are flavored salts, spiced salts, smoked salts, and salts of the most beautiful hues. We use this magical ingredient in everything; whether it's for sprinkling over an omelet or decorating the rim of a margarita glass.

We season, preserve, bake, cure, brine, pickle, and make rubs with this wonderful ingredient. Harvested from land and sea it comes in a multitude of shapes, textures, colors, and tastes. Just a sprinkle of this divine substance can make a dish sing.

Cooks delight in their collections of salts from all over the world. They love to discuss the effects of salt and how they use it to add a freshness and piquancy to food. Some people with a strong devotion to salt even go so far as to carry around a small salt cellar with them.

Salt has been a prized possession since the beginning of civilization. It was once used as a form of currency and wars have been won and lost over it. Nations have been taxed on their salt. In China, salt tax revenues were used to build the Great Wall. The Greeks and the Mayans worshipped their gods with salt offerings. Roman soldiers were given an allowance of salt known as "salarium," from which the word "salary" comes. There are salt routes all over the world that were used to transport salt from continent to continent. In Italy one of the oldest roads is called Via Salaria, meaning salt route, and Venice has a long history of making herbed salts. At one time salt was so precious it was traded ounce for ounce with gold.

So where does the salt that we buy from our local market come from? It is mined deep in the earth and harvested from salt lakes or salt pans. Salt lakes are naturally occurring inland bodies of water, which are remnants of ancient seas. Salt pans are man-made basins, situated next to the sea, which are flooded with salt waters. These in turn evaporate in the sun and the salt that is left behind is harvested.

Wherever it comes from in the world we are always surprised and delighted to have it around.

Remember if you spill salt, throw a few granules over your shoulder for good luck.

Salt directory

1 Rock salt
This is mined from salt deposits deep in the earth and is sometimes colored with minerals. It has a large grain, which makes it ideal for use when cooking with a salt crust, but otherwise it is usually put in a salt grinder for easier use.

2 Murray River salt flakes
These delicate pink salt flakes come from the Murray River region in Australia. They are harvested from pure underground saline waters rich in minerals, giving it its wonderful taste and pink color. Good for cooking and as a pretty garnish.

3 Himalayan pink rock salt
This salt is hand-mined in Nepal from ancient salt deposits and is believed to be the purest salt on earth. The iron content gives it its distinct pink color. Fun to have in a block and grate over food.

4 Green tea salt
This salt is made by mixing Matcha, a Japanese green tea powder, with sea salt and grinding it to a fine powder using a mortar and pestle. It adds a gentle taste when sprinkled on salads and is high in amino acids.

5 Smoked salts
Smoked salts are man-made by smoking the salts with flavored wood chips. They come in versions such as mesquite or hickory and add a deep flavor to dishes.

6 Hawaiian black lava sea salt
Harvested sea salt is mixed with crushed black lava and black charcoal which gives it its dark color. It should be sprinkled on food only at the last minute. Do not immerse it in liquid as it will lose its color in the process.

7 Sea salt flakes
These are large delicate salt crystals made from the evaporation by the sun on the sea or salt lakes. Rich in minerals, they come in an array of colors depending on their geographical origin.

8 Hawaiian red alaea sea salt
This salt hails from the island of Kauai. "Alaea" is the name given to the natural mineral found in the runoff from the volcano, which occurs in the rainy season. It is a red clay which colors the salt pans a deep burnt red color. This salt is used mostly for garnishing dishes.

9 Sel gris
Sel gris, gray salt, is also known as Celtic sea salt. Hand-harvested from the bottom of the salt flats in Guérande, France, it gets its grey color from the clay in the beds.

10 Jurassic salt
Jurassic salt gets its name from the era 150 million years ago when Utah was mostly under water. When the water dried up, it left behind this mineral-intense salt with a pinkish hue. This salt has a delicate flavor and is perfect for most types of cooking, especially baking.

11 Fleur de sel
A hand-harvested sea salt from the Guérande and Camargue regions in France. The crystallized salt is skimmed from the surface of the saltpans, flooded with the waters of the Atlantic. It has a mild flavor.

12 Flavored salts
These salts are made with fruits, spices (for example saffron), fresh and dried herbs, pounded together with salt using a mortar and pestle. If you use fresh herbs or fruits, crush then spread them out on a baking sheet and place in a low temperature oven for 30 minutes.

Appetizers

Potatoes, truffles, and salt are a match made in heaven. Use a mandolin to slice the potatoes wafer thin.

Gold potato chips
with truffle salt

1 lb. Yukon Gold potatoes or similar (about 6 small), skin on
vegetable oil, for deep-frying
truffle salt, to sprinkle

an electric deep-fat fryer
a deep-frying thermometer

SERVES 4–6

Wash and dry the potatoes, slice thinly, and set aside.

Heat the oil in the deep-fat fryer or a heavy-bottomed pan until it reaches 350°F. To test if the oil is hot enough, drop a cube of bread in the oil and it should turn golden brown in about 20 seconds.

Fry the potato slices in batches and drain on paper towels.

Put the drained potato crisps in a bowl, sprinkle with the truffle salt, toss, and serve.

You can't watch a movie without snacks. My popcorn has a fabulous pink tint and chili kick. One in every dozen Padron peppers has a fiery hit, so be prepared with a glass of cold beer to hand.

Fun popcorn *with chili salt*

4 tablespoons Murray River salt flakes
2 tablespoons chipotle chili powder, or to taste
2 bags unsalted microwave popcorn

SERVES 4

In a small bowl, mix together the salt and chili powder. Cook the popcorn according to the instructions on the packet. When it has popped, put in a large bowl, sprinkle with the chili salt, and toss to mix.

Padron peppers

¼ cup olive oil
1 lb. Padron peppers
sel gris

SERVES 4–6

Put a sauté pan over high heat. When it starts to smoke, turn the heat down to medium. Add the olive oil and swirl the pan once to cover the bottom with oil.

Add the peppers and cook until slightly blistered, stirring occasionally. Empty the hot peppers into a bowl and sprinkle generously with the sel gris.

Candied salted almonds

2 cups raw almonds, skin on
½ cup dark brown sugar
¼ cup maple syrup
1 teaspoon chipotle chili powder
1 tablespoon sel gris,
    coarsely ground

MAKES 2 CUPS

Preheat the oven to 375°F.

Mix all the ingredients except for the sel gris together in a bowl until the almonds are well coated. Spread the almonds on a nonstick baking sheet and bake in the preheated oven for 5–8 minutes. The sugars will bubble and turn a darker color.

Remove the almonds from the oven and stir with a wooden spoon. Sprinkle with sel gris and set aside to cool on the baking sheet. As they cool, the sugars will begin to harden.

When the almonds have cooled, serve them in a bowl. The nuts can be stored in an airtight container for a week at room temperature. These spicy, sweet, and salty nuts are delicious sprinkled over salads or mixed into a pilaf.

Corsican fried olives

4 oz. goat cheese, room temperature
1 teaspoon herbes de Provence
finely grated zest of 1 orange
1 egg
1 tablespoon all-purpose flour
1 cup panko or coarse bread crumbs
40 large green and black olives,
    pitted
2 cups vegetable oil
fleur de sel, to sprinkle

a pastry bag with a small tip
a deep-frying thermometer

MAKES 40

In a bowl mix together the goat cheese, herbs, and orange zest until smooth. Put the mixture in the pastry bag and set aside.

Lightly beat the egg in a small bowl and set aside. Put the flour on a small plate and the bread crumbs on another.

Using the pastry bag, pipe each olive full with the cheese mixture. Dip each olive in the flour, then the egg, and toss in the bread crumbs until well coated.

Heat the oil in a heavy-bottomed pan until the oil reaches 350°F on a deep-frying thermometer.

Alternatively, test the oil by dropping in a cube of bread. It should turn golden brown in about 20 seconds.

Fry the olives in batches until crispy and golden brown, for about 1 minute. Drain on paper towels. Sprinkle generously with the fleur de sel and serve.

Spiced and marinated olives

1 dried red chile
¼ cup Spanish salted Marcona
    almonds
1 cup green olives
3 kumquats
½ teaspoon cumin seeds
¼ cup Spanish olive oil

MAKES 2 CUPS

Roughly chop the chile and the almonds and put them in a bowl with the olives.

Thinly slice the kumquats and add to the olive mixture. Sprinkle with cumin seeds, pour over the olive oil, and mix thoroughly. Set aside for at least 1 hour before serving to let the flavors blend.

Here is a fun spin on *bacalhau*, the famous Portuguese salt cod fritters. I like to make a rich green olive salsa to pile on top. Look for green olives marinated in herbs; they have a deep earthy flavor and when combined with the latkes bring all the flavors of the Mediterranean together. When buying the salt cod, make sure the flesh is pure white.

Salt cod latkes *with green olive salsa*

1 lb. salt cod
1 lb. russet potatoes, or similar starchy potatoes
2 tablespoons fresh oregano leaves, roughly chopped
2 tablespoons chive onions or scallions, chopped
1 garlic clove, finely chopped
1 egg, lightly beaten
freshly ground black pepper
olive oil, for frying

Green olive salsa
12 herbed green olives such as Picholine, pitted
1 tablespoon finely grated lemon zest
2 tablespoons olive oil

MAKES 24

Put the salt cod in a bowl and cover with cold water. Place in the refrigerator for 2 days, changing the water 4 times a day. This will rehydrate the cod and remove any excess salt.

When the cod is ready, drain, put in a pot, and cover with cold water. Bring to a boil and cook for 15 minutes until the cod begins to break away from the skin and bones. Remove from the heat, drain, and cool. Using a fork, flake the fish, discarding the skin and bones. Mash and set aside.

Peel and roughly grate the potatoes. In a large bowl mix together the cod, potatoes, oregano, chive onions or scallions, garlic, and egg. Season with black pepper and set the latke mixture aside.

To make the Green Olive Salsa, roughly chop the herbed green olives and put in a small bowl. Add the lemon zest along with the olive oil and mix thoroughly.

Heat a medium-sized nonstick sauté pan over medium to high heat and drizzle with enough olive oil to fry the latkes. Drop heaping tablespoons of the latke mixture into the sauté pan.

Cook the latkes for 2–3 minutes on each side until crispy and golden brown and the potato is cooked. Repeat in batches until you have used all the mixture.

Arrange the latkes on a serving plate, top with a little salsa, and serve.

Traditional suppli have mozzarella inside and are known in Rome as *suppli al telefono*, because when you bite into them the mozzarella pulls and looks like a telephone wire. I hide a cured black olive in the center of mine, which makes for a delicious surprise. It's a great party dish for the winter, and also a marvelous way to use up any leftover risotto.

Olive suppli

17 cured black olives, pitted
¼ cup all-purpose flour
2 eggs, beaten
1½ cups bread crumbs
vegetable oil, for frying
saffron salt, to sprinkle

Risotto
½ cup dried porcini mushrooms
1 cup white wine
2 cups chicken stock
2 tablespoons olive oil
1 garlic clove, finely chopped
2 tablespoons thyme leaves
1 tablespoon chopped fresh
  rosemary
1 cup arborio rice
½ cup grated Parmesan cheese
cracked black pepper and sea salt

a deep-frying thermometer

MAKES 17

For the risotto, soak the mushrooms in the wine for 30 minutes. Drain, reserving the liquid, and chop roughly. Pour the reserved liquid into a small pan with the chicken stock. Bring to a boil and reduce to a simmer.

Put the olive oil, garlic, thyme, rosemary, and mushrooms in a medium pan and cook over medium to high heat for a few seconds, coating with the olive oil. Add the rice and stir for 2–3 minutes until well coated and translucent. Start adding the stock a ladleful at a time, stirring continuously until the liquid has been absorbed. Continue until you have used all the liquid, about 20 minutes. Stir in the cheese and season with cracked black pepper and sea salt. Pour onto a large plate and spread out to cool.

To make the suppli, take tablespoons of cooled risotto and form 17 balls. With your forefinger make a dent in each risotto ball and place an olive in the center. Roll the risotto ball in your hand to reshape and cover the olive.

Dust the suppli balls with flour, dip into the beaten egg, and then toss in the bread crumbs until well coated. At this stage they can be left to rest in the refrigerator for up to 6 hours until you are ready to cook.

Heat the oil in a heavy-bottomed pan until the oil reaches 350°F on a deep-frying thermometer. Alternatively, test the oil by dropping in a cube of bread. It should turn golden brown in about 20 seconds.

Fry the suppli in batches until crispy and golden brown, about 2 minutes. Drain on paper towels. Sprinkle generously with saffron salt and serve.

I love this dip made with goat milk yogurt. It is perfect as a light snack in warm weather, served with pita chips, cut raw vegetables, or bread. Alternatively, a large dollop turns a simple fish cake into something special.

Goat cheese dip
with citrus salt

2 lbs. goat milk yogurt, preferably organic

extra virgin olive oil, to drizzle

Citrus salt
finely grated zest of 1 unwaxed lemon

2 tablespoons rock salt granules

a cheesecloth square

MAKES 2 CUPS

Line a strainer with cheesecloth. You can also use a single layer of paper towels or a coffee filter.

Rest the lined strainer on the rim of a bowl deep enough to catch the drained fluid. Empty the goat milk yogurt into the lined sieve, cover with plastic wrap, and leave in the refrigerator overnight.

Make the Citrus Salt by pounding the lemon zest and salt in a mortar and pestle. Transfer to a small bowl.

The next day, remove the goat cheese from the fridge and discard the liquid. To serve, put the cheese in a serving bowl. Drizzle with olive oil and sprinkle with the Citrus Salt.

This is a pretty dish to look at as well as being very tasty. The beautiful orange flesh and dark red skins of the garnet sweet potatoes are offset by the ochre-colored salt. Hawaiian red alaea sea salt is a garnishing salt only, rich in minerals, which give it such a vivid color. When cooked, it loses both its color and flavor.

Roasted sweet potato wedges
with Hawaiian alaea sea salt

2 lbs. garnet sweet potatoes (about 3), skin on

¼ cup olive oil

cracked black pepper

Hawaiian red alaea sea salt

SERVES 4

Preheat the oven to 375°F.

Rinse and dry the sweet potatoes. Cut them into thick wedges and arrange on a nonstick baking sheet. Pour the olive oil over them, tossing the wedges to make sure they are evenly coated. Season with cracked black pepper.

Bake in the preheated oven for 10 minutes. Turn the wedges over and return to the oven for another 10–15 minutes, until golden brown and crispy on the edges. Pierce the wedges with a sharp knife to make sure they are cooked through.

Remove from the oven, sprinkle generously with Hawaiian red alaea sea salt, and serve.

I like to make gazpacho with heirloom tomatoes of different colors, but if you can't find them, use any very ripe and tasty tomatoes. The sherry vinegar is the key to gazpacho, so seek out a heady one from Jerez in Spain—it will make all the difference.

Gazpacho *with smoked salted croutons*

3 lbs. heirloom tomatoes
1 garlic clove
1 small red onion
2 Persian cucumbers
1 green bell pepper
1 Serrano chile (red or green)
¼ cup extra virgin olive oil
¼ cup Jerez sherry vinegar
sel gris and cracked black pepper
olive oil, to drizzle

Smoked salted croutons
1 small baguette
1 garlic clove, finely chopped
¼ cup olive oil
1 tablespoon smoked sea salt

a 6-cup food processor

SERVES 4

To peel the tomatoes, fill a small bowl with ice and water and set aside. Bring a medium-sized pot of water to a boil. Using a sharp knife, score a cross in the top of each tomato. Drop the tomatoes into the hot water for 30 seconds. Remove with a slotted spoon and drop into the iced water for 1 minute. Remove from the water and peel. Cut the tomatoes in half or quarters, depending on the size, and put in the food processor.

Roughly chop the garlic, onion, and cucumbers and add to the tomatoes. Cut the green pepper and Serrano chile in half and remove the white pith and seeds. Chop and add to the tomatoes. Pulse the tomato mixture until it is chunky. Pour the gazpacho into a large bowl and stir in the olive oil and Jerez sherry vinegar. Season with sel gris and cracked black pepper then chill in the refrigerator until ready to serve.

Preheat the oven to 400°F.

To make the Smoked Salted Croutons, slice the baguette lengthwise into 4 and lay the slices on a baking sheet. Mix the garlic and olive oil in a small bowl and drizzle over the bread. Sprinkle with the smoked sea salt and bake in the preheated oven for 8–10 minutes until golden.

Pour the gazpacho into 4 bowls and drizzle with olive oil. Serve with the Smoked Salted Croutons.

Entrées

Rubbing kosher salt over the duck draws excess moisture out of the skin, while scalding makes for a crispy skin when roasted. A wonderful honey-spiced glaze adds a vibrant color and flavor to the meat.

Crispy roast duck *with Asian greens*

1 fresh duck, 3 lbs.
3 tablespoons kosher salt

Honey glaze
4 star anise, crushed
⅓ cup plus 1 tablespoon honey
1 teaspoon ground cinnamon
finely grated zest of 1 orange and
    freshly squeezed juice of ½ orange
    (reserve both orange halves for
    stuffing the duck)
1 teaspoon Sichuan crushed
    peppercorns
2 tablespoons soy sauce
1 inch piece fresh ginger, grated
2 red Thai chiles, chopped
2 tablespoons dark brown sugar

Asian greens
3 tablespoons peanut oil
2 tablespoons toasted sesame oil
2 tablespoons red wine vinegar
1 teaspoon soy sauce
1 teaspoon honey
3 cups mixed Asian salad greens
cracked black pepper and green
    tea salt

a roasting pan lined with foil
a roasting rack

SERVES 4

Wash and dry the duck. Rub the kosher salt all over the duck skin, cover, and leave in the refrigerator overnight.

Put the roasting rack on the lined roasting pan. Bring a kettle of water to a boil. Put the duck in a large bowl and pour boiling water over it. Immediately remove the duck from the bowl and place on the roasting rack in the roasting pan. Set aside.

Preheat the oven to 400°F.

Stuff the duck with the orange halves. Mix all the Honey Glaze ingredients together in a bowl and brush over the duck. Roast in the preheated oven for 30 minutes, remove from the oven, and drain off the fat that has accumulated in the bottom of the pan. You may need to cover the tips of the wings with foil, as they will be very crispy. Turn the oven down to 375°F and put the duck back in the oven for another 30 minutes.

Remove the duck from the oven and let it rest for 15 minutes in a warm place.

To prepare the Asian Greens, whisk the peanut oil, sesame oil, red wine vinegar, soy sauce, and honey together. Season with the cracked black pepper and green tea salt. Put the salad greens in a bowl and toss with the dressing.

Carve the duck and serve with the salad.

Brining the poussins ensures a crispy skin when roasted. You can use any tea to make the brine, but jasmine tea infuses a floral taste into the poussins and creates a subtle flavor when cooked. Serve with the dark green salsa verde. You can also make this with Cornish game hen.

Jasmine-brined roasted poussins *with salsa verde*

2 poussins (or 1 Cornish game hen)
1 small unwaxed lemon
1 garlic clove, minced
1 tablespoon olive oil
sea salt and cracked black pepper

Brining solution
4 tablespoons jasmine tea or
    4 jasmine teabags
6 cups boiling water
¼ cup coarse rock salt
1 tablespoon dark brown sugar

Salsa verde
1 cup Italian parsley leaves
1 cup cilantro leaves
1 cup mint leaves
2 garlic cloves, finely chopped
finely grated zest of 1 small unwaxed
    lemon (see method)
1 tablespoon brined capers
½ cup olive oil

a roasting pan, kitchen twine

SERVES 2

First make the brine. Put the jasmine tea in a large measuring jug and pour over the boiling water. Add the salt and sugar and stir until dissolved. Set aside to cool completely.

Wash and dry the poussins and put in a deep dish. Pour the cooled brine over them, cover, and refrigerate for 6–8 hours.

When you are ready to cook, preheat the oven to 375°F. Remove the poussins from the brining mixture and pat dry, removing any leftover tea leaves. Discard the brining mixture; it cannot be used again.

Place the poussins in a roasting pan. Zest the lemon and reserve for use in the Salsa Verde. Cut the lemon into quarters and stuff the cavity with them. Tie the legs together with kitchen twine. Mix together the garlic and oil and rub over the skin of the poussins. Season with sea salt and cracked black pepper.

Roast in the preheated oven for 35 minutes until cooked and the poussin juices run clear.

To make the Salsa Verde, put all the salsa ingredients in a food processor and pulse until roughly chopped. Be careful not to overprocess; you want the salsa to be slightly chunky. Season with sea salt and black pepper.

When the poussins are ready, remove from the oven and set aside to rest for 10 minutes, covered with aluminum foil, in a warm place. Carve and serve with the Salsa Verde.

This chicken dish is so easy to prepare. You will be amazed at how beautifully succulent it is, as the salt crust keeps all the moisture in during cooking. As you are using egg whites to help bind the salt, save the yolks and make aïoli or mayonnaise to go with cold leftovers.

Mustard and herb chicken *baked in a salt crust*

1 chicken, 3½–4 lbs.
1 lemon, cut in half
3 tablespoons Dijon mustard
1 tablespoon herbes de Provence
5 egg whites
4 lbs. coarse sea salt
cracked black pepper

a roasting pan or baking dish similar
   in size to the chicken

SERVES 6

Preheat the oven to 375°F.

Stuff the chicken with the lemon halves and rub the mustard all over the skin. Sprinkle with the herbes de Provence and season with cracked black pepper. Set the chicken aside.

In a large bowl lightly beat the egg whites until frothy. Add the salt and mix thoroughly. The mixture should be the consistency of wet sand.

Spread a thin layer of salt evenly on the bottom of the roasting pan or baking dish. Put the chicken on top and cover with the rest of the salt mixture. Pat down well and make sure there are no holes from which the steam can escape.

Bake the chicken in the preheated oven for 1 hour. You'll notice that the salt will turn a golden brown. Remove the chicken from the oven and let it rest for 10 minutes.

Using the back of a knife, crack open the crust and remove. Put the chicken on a plate or wooden board and carve.

This is a simple way to cook lamb—coat it in a thick crust and roast it in the oven. The aromas from the spices are intoxicating, especially the fresh curry leaves hidden in the crust.

Indian spiced leg of lamb
cooked in a salt crust, with raita

3 lb. leg of lamb, bone in
4 garlic cloves, sliced

Spice rub
20 green cardamom pods, bashed
1 teaspoon cumin seeds
1 cinnamon stick, broken into pieces
½ teaspoon whole cloves
½ teaspoon turmeric
½ teaspoon chipotle chili powder
½ teaspoon Spanish smoked paprika
2 tablespoons olive oil

Salt crust
2½ cups coarse sea salt
3½ cups all-purpose flour
1 small bunch fresh curry leaves

Raita
1 cup plain yogurt
2 garlic cloves, finely chopped
1 small cucumber, grated
2 tablespoons fresh mint leaves, torn
sea salt
ground sumac, to sprinkle

a lightly oiled roasting pan

SERVES 6–8

Wash the leg of lamb and pat dry. Using a sharp knife, stab the lamb all over and stud with the slices of garlic. Set the lamb aside.

Put all the dry ingredients for the Spice Rub in a saucepan and dry roast over low heat, stirring continuously until they are lightly toasted. Pound the toasted spices to a rough mixture using a mortar and pestle. Add the olive oil and stir to a paste. Spread the paste all over the lamb and chill in the refrigerator for at least 2 hours or for up to 24 hours.

When you are ready to cook the lamb, preheat the oven to 400°F.

To make the Salt Crust, mix the salt, flour, and curry leaves together in a bowl with 1 cup water to give a doughy consistency. If the mixture is too dry, add more water 1 tablespoon at a time. Roll out on a floured worktop to twice the size of the lamb. Put the lamb leg at one end of the pastry and fold over the remaining dough. Seal, making sure there are no holes for any steam to escape. Put in a lightly oiled roasting pan and bake in the preheated oven for 1 hour.

Take the lamb out of the oven and let rest for 10–15 minutes.

To make the Raita, mix together the yogurt, garlic, grated cucumber, and mint leaves. Season with sea salt and sprinkle with the sumac. Refrigerate until needed.

To serve the lamb, peel off the crust and place on a large plate or wooden board to carve. Serve with the Raita.

1 lb. pork tenderloin
cilantro leaves and lime wedges,
    to garnish

Spicy marinade
2 tablespoons rice wine vinegar
2 green chiles, chopped
1 tablespoon Kecap Manis (thick
    medium-sweet soy sauce)
1 large garlic clove, finely chopped
1 tablespoon toasted sesame oil
2 tablespoons fish sauce
2 tablespoons peanut oil
2 tablespoons chopped cilantro leaves
1 tablespoon grated fresh ginger

Roast salted peanut sauce
1 tablespoon peanut oil
1 garlic clove, finely chopped
2 red Thai chiles, finely chopped
4 kaffir lime leaves
1 stalk lemon grass, cut into 4
1 teaspoon garam masala or
    curry powder
2 tablespoons dark brown sugar
1 cup Salty Peanut Butter (see
    page 60)
1 cup coconut milk
¼ cup unsweetened coconut flakes
finely grated zest and freshly
    squeezed juice of 1 lime
2 tablespoons fish sauce

18–20 bamboo skewers, soaked in
    cold water for 30 minutes
a ridged stove-top grill pan

MAKES 18–20 SKEWERS

These spicy pork skewers dipped in peanut sauce are
heaven on a stick. They are great for weekend get-togethers,
when you want to make delicious, easy food with minimum
kitchen time. You can also pop these on a barbecue grill
and forgo the stove top.

Spicy pork satay
with roast salted peanut sauce

Slice the pork into ¼-inch pieces and put in a bowl. Mix together all
the Spicy Marinade ingredients and pour over the pork. Cover and put
in the refrigerator for 30 minutes.

To make the Roast Salted Peanut Sauce, heat the peanut oil in a
saucepan over medium heat. Sauté the garlic, chiles, kaffir lime
leaves, lemon grass, and garam masala for 2 minutes. Add the sugar
and stir. Now add the Salty Peanut Butter, coconut milk, coconut flakes,
along with the lime zest and juice. Cook for 15 minutes. Take off the heat
and stir in the fish sauce. Pour the mixture into a bowl and set aside.

Remove the pork from the refrigerator and thread onto the soaked
bamboo skewers.

Heat the grill pan over high heat until nearly smoking. Grill the pork
skewers for 3–4 minutes each side until brown and caramelized.

Garnish the pork skewers with cilantro leaves and serve with lime
wedges and the Roast Salted Peanut Sauce.

This is a showstopper at any dinner party. Crack open the salt crust
at the table and let your guests be dazzled by the heavenly aromas
and the bright pink shells.

Salt-crusted citrus shrimp *with chili dipping sauce*

finely grated zest and freshly
   squeezed juice of 2 limes
4 lbs. coarse sea salt
1 lb. large shrimp, unshelled

Chili dipping sauce
2 red chiles, finely chopped
4 kaffir lime leaves, finely shredded
1 scallion, finely chopped
1 garlic clove, finely chopped
½ cup fish sauce
finely grated zest and freshly
   squeezed juice of 2 limes
1 tablespoon rice wine vinegar
1 tablespoon brown sugar
1 tablespoon peanuts, chopped

SERVES 4

Preheat the oven to 475°F.

In a large bowl mix together the lime zest and juice, salt, and 1 cup water.
The mixture should be the consistency of wet sand. Spread a layer of the
salt mixture in a baking dish and arrange the shrimp on top. Cover with
the remaining salt mixture and pat well down, making sure the shrimp
are completely covered and there are no gaps anywhere.

Bake in the preheated oven for 15 minutes. The salt should be slightly
golden on top.

Whisk together all the Chili Dipping Sauce ingredients until the sugar
has dissolved. Divide between 4 small bowls.

When the shrimp are ready, take them out of the oven and let them rest
for 5 minutes. Using the back of a knife, crack open the crust and remove
the top part. Serve at the table.

Let guests help themselves, peel their own shrimp, and dip in the chili
sauce. Have a large empty bowl handy for the shells.

Miso is a traditional staple of Japanese cooking. It is made by fermenting soybeans in sea salt, which results in a thick paste. Most common are white, yellow, and red miso. The delicate, slightly salty and fruity flavor of yellow miso really enhances the flavor of wild salmon. This is a fantastic easy supper dish and healthy, too.

Miso and nut-crusted salmon

2 x 8 oz. wild salmon fillets,
    center cut
1 tablespoon olive oil
chopped chive onions, to garnish

Miso and nut topping
1 tablespoon yellow miso paste
½ cup cashews, roughly chopped
½ red Serrano chile, finely chopped
finely grated zest and freshly
    squeezed juice of 1 lime
1 tablespoon toasted sesame oil

SERVES 2

Preheat the oven to 400°F.

Rinse and dry the salmon. Drizzle the olive oil into a small baking dish and place the salmon fillets in it.

To make the Miso and Nut Topping, mix together the miso, cashews, chile, lime zest and juice, and sesame oil. Divide the mixture and spread on top of the salmon fillets.

Cook in the preheated oven for 12–15 minutes until the fish is cooked and the topping is golden brown.

Garnish with chopped chive onions and serve.

It seems everyone has a favorite way of making this classic. My overnight version is quick compared with the traditional method of curing for several days. Wild salmon makes a huge difference; if it's not available, use organic farmed salmon. The gravadlax will keep for 5 days in the refrigerator.

Gravadlax

1 cup coarse sea salt
½ cup brown sugar
2 tablespoons juniper berries
2 tablespoons black peppercorns, crushed
3 bunches fresh dill
2½ lbs. wild salmon fillet, boned and with skin on (this is 1 side of a whole salmon)
¼ cup gin
lemon wedges, to serve

Caper sauce
1 cup crème fraîche
2 tablespoons salt
2 tablespoons cornichons
1 tablespoon salted capers
finely grated zest and freshly squeezed juice of 1 unwaxed lemon

a prepared baking sheet or dish (see method)

SERVES 8

You will need a baking sheet or shallow dish that will accommodate the salmon. Line the bottom of this with plastic wrap.

Crush the juniper berries and black peppercorns using a mortar and pestle.

In a bowl mix together the salt, brown sugar, along with the crushed peppercorns and juniper berries. Sprinkle half the salt mixture on top of the prepared baking sheet or dish and spread 1 bunch of dill over the salt mixture. Place the salmon, skin side down, on top of the dill and drizzle with the gin. Cover the salmon with the remainder of the salt mixture and then top with the remaining dill.

Cover the salmon with plastic wrap, making sure it is airtight. Next, you need to put a weight on the salmon; a heavy saucepan or pizza stone is ideal. Put the salmon in the refrigerator overnight to cure for 12 hours.

To make the Caper Sauce, put all the ingredients in a food processor and pulse until roughly chopped. Transfer to a bowl, cover, and refrigerate.

Unwrap the salmon and remove the dill. Place the salmon on a wooden board. Using the back of a knife, scrape off the salt mixture.

To serve, cut the salmon as thinly as possible in diagonal slices. Serve with the caper sauce, lemon wedges, and a crusty baguette.

Branzino is also known as Mediterranean sea bass. It is a white flaky fish with a sweetish taste. You could use any firm fish for this recipe. I like to include fennel seeds in the crust to add an extra layer of flavor.

Salt-crusted branzino

1 whole branzino, about
   2 lbs., cleaned
2 branches fresh rosemary
1 lemon, sliced
½ fennel bulb, thinly sliced
1 garlic clove, thinly sliced
¼ cup white wine
5 egg whites
6 cups coarse sea salt or rock salt
4 tablespoons fennel seeds
cracked black pepper
1 lemon, cut into wedges, to serve

SERVES 2

Preheat the oven to 425°F.

Wash the fish and pat dry. Stuff the fish with the rosemary, lemon slices, fennel, and garlic. Drizzle with the white wine.

In a large bowl, lightly whisk the egg whites. Add the salt and fennel seeds and mix until it is the consistency of wet sand. Spread half the salt mixture in the bottom of a baking dish and lay the fish on top. Season with cracked black pepper. Cover the fish with the remainder of the salt and pack tightly, making sure there are no holes for the steam to escape.

Bake in the preheated oven for 30 minutes, then remove and allow the fish to rest untouched for another 5 minutes. Crack open the salt crust with the back of a knife and remove the salt from around the fish. Serve with lemon wedges.

This is a delightfully pretty and refreshing salad in which the olive salt brings out the sweetness of the watermelon. Ricotta salata, a lightly salted cheese made from sheep milk, originates from the island of Sicily. If you can't find a mini watermelon, buy the smallest available and cut it in half. You can use feta cheese if ricotta salata isn't available.

Watermelon and ricotta salata salad *with olive salt*

1 mini seedless watermelon
6 oz. ricotta salata cheese
2 tablespoons fresh oregano leaves
olive oil, to drizzle
freshly ground black pepper

Olive salt
10 black olives, pitted
2½ tablespoons sea salt

SERVES 2

Peel the watermelon and cut it into bite-size chunks. Put in a serving bowl, crumble the ricotta salata over the watermelon, and sprinkle with the oregano.

To make the Olive Salt, chop the olives roughly. Grind them with the salt using a mortar and pestle until the olives are mashed.

Drizzle the olive oil over the salad and season with black pepper. Sprinkle with a generous amount of the olive salt. Put the remainder of the salt in a bowl to use on other dishes.

Summer, when peaches are in season, is the time to make this salad. The sweet and juicy peaches play off the slightly salty mozzarella, and a sprinkle of curry salt spices up the whole dish.

Peach caprese *with curry salt*

2 x 8 oz. fresh buffalo
   mozzarella balls
2 large yellow peaches
1 small bunch fresh mint
1 small bunch fresh basil

Vinaigrette
¼ cup champagne vinegar
½ cup extra virgin olive oil
½ teaspoon honey

Curry salt
2 tablespoons fleur de sel
2 teaspoons Madras curry powder

SERVES 4

Slice the mozzarella balls into ¼-inch pieces. Cut the peaches in half and remove the pits. Slice the peach halves into ¼-inch pieces. Tear the basil leaves and mint leaves from their stems, reserving 4 sprigs of mint for the garnish.

To make the Vinaigrette, put all the ingredients in a small bowl and whisk together.

To make the Curry Salt, mix together the fleur de sel and curry powder in a small bowl.

To assemble the salad, line up 4 salad plates. Put a slice of mozzarella on each plate, then top with a slice of peach. Add a few basil and mint leaves and continue to layer.

Drizzle the Vinaigrette over the salads and finish with a sprinkle of Curry Salt. Garnish with a sprig of mint.

This is the perfect dish to serve with fish. It's delicious and simple, with the added bonus of the wonderful aroma of rosemary while it's cooking. Use tiny black Niçoise olives—their intense flavor goes very well with the sweetness of the tomatoes.

Roasted cherry tomatoes
with olives and fleur de sel

1 sprig fresh rosemary
1 lb. cherry tomatoes
½ cup Niçoise olives, pitted

cracked black pepper and fleur de sel

SERVES 4

Preheat the oven to 375°F.

Run your fingers down the rosemary sprig, tearing the leaves off as you go. It will yield about 2 tablespoons of leaves.

In a bowl toss together the rosemary, tomatoes, and olives. Season with cracked black pepper.

Pour the tomato mixture onto a nonstick baking sheet or pan. Roast in the preheated oven for 10 minutes, until the tomatoes have some color and have softened. Remove from the oven and shake the pan. Set aside to cool for a few minutes.

Put the tomatoes in a bowl, sprinkle with the fleur de sel, and serve.

Cook corn cobs on the barbecue, tear off the outer husks, and slather them in smoked pimento butter to enjoy the deep, smoky, soulful flavors. Leftover butter will go well with any grilled meat. You can keep it in the refrigerator for up to 1 week.

Barbecue corn on the cob
with smoked pimento butter

2 sticks unsalted butter, room temperature
2 teaspoons sweet smoked paprika

1 teaspoon smoked sea salt
6 corn on the cob, husks still on

SERVES 6

Put the butter in a food processor with the paprika and smoked sea salt. Mix until the butter is smooth. Refrigerate until ready to use.

Preheat a barbecue grill.

Put the corn cobs, with the husks still on, on the hot barbecue grill. Cook for 3 minutes, turn over, and cook for another 3 minutes. You want the corn to have a crunch when you bite into it.

When the corn is ready, remove from the heat and tear back the outer husk. You can use the husk as a handle. Spread the Smoked Pimento Butter over the corn and eat immediately.

Sides

Pretzel bites

1 cup warm water
2 tablespoons salted butter, room temperature, in small cubes
3 teaspoons rapid-rise yeast (instant yeast)
1 teaspoon white sugar
2¾ cups all-purpose flour

4 teaspoons baking powder
rock salt flakes, for topping
American hot dog mustard, to serve (optional)

MAKES ABOUT 40

In a glass measuring jug, mix together the warm water, butter, yeast, and sugar. Stir until the butter has melted.

To make the dough, put the flour in a food processor. With the motor running, add the liquid to the flour in a steady stream until all the liquid is incorporated and the dough forms a ball, about 3 minutes. Add a little extra flour if necessary. Put the dough on a floured worktop and knead for 2 minutes. Form into a ball and put in an oiled bowl. Cover with a kitchen towel and let prove in a warm place for 1 hour.

Preheat the oven to 425°F.

Turn the dough out onto a floured worktop and roll into a 12 x 6 inch rectangle. With a sharp knife, cut 1-inch strips of dough from the long side. Take these dough strands and cut into 1-inch bite-size pieces. (To make the classic pretzel shape, shape the dough strands into a figure of 8, then continue as below.)

In a nonstick wok or pan (do not use aluminum), bring the baking powder to a boil with 4 cups water. Drop the dough pieces into the water for about 1 minute and remove with a slotted spoon onto nonstick baking sheets. They will puff up. This brining procedure gives the pretzel its slightly hard chewy outside, while the inside remains soft.

Sprinkle the rock salt over the pretzel bites and bake in the preheated oven for 10–15 minutes until brown on top. Serve with American mustard, if desired.

Parmesan and sage wafers

1 cup grated Parmesan cheese
1 tablespoon finely chopped fresh sage

coarse black pepper
Himalayan pink rock salt

MAKES 14

Preheat the oven to 350°F.

Mix together the Parmesan cheese and sage and season with black pepper. Drop tablespoons of the mixture at 2-inch intervals on a nonstick baking sheet. Pat down the mounds with your fingers. Bake in the preheated oven for 5–6 minutes until the mixture is completely melted and the edges are turning golden brown. Keep an eye on them as they brown fast.

Remove the wafers from the oven and let stand for a few moments to firm up. They will be soft when they come out of the oven but harden as they cool.

With a spatula carefully remove the wafers and leave to cool completely on a wire rack. Once they have cooled, sprinkle with Himalayan pink rock salt. They can be stored in an airtight container for 2 days. These delicate lacy wafers are ideal with a glass of prosecco, or try them instead of croutons on a Caesar salad.

Extra-long Hawaiian black salted breadsticks

3½ cups all-purpose flour

1⅓ cups warm water

3 tablespoons olive oil

1 tablespoon milk

3 teaspoons rapid-rise yeast (instant yeast)

½ teaspoon brown sugar

¼ cup olive oil

¼ cup Hawaiian black lava sea salt

MAKES ABOUT 24

To make the dough, put the flour in a food processor. In a glass measuring jug mix together the warm water, olive oil, milk, yeast, and brown sugar.

With the motor running, add the liquid to the flour in a steady stream. Process until all the liquid is incorporated and the dough forms a ball, about 3 minutes. Transfer the dough to a floured worktop and knead for about 3 minutes. Form into a ball and put in an oiled bowl. Cover with a kitchen towel and let prove in a warm place until it doubles in size.

Preheat the oven to 425°F.

Turn the dough out onto a floured surface. Roll into a rectangle, 15 x 10 inches, and ¼ inch thick. Use a sharp knife to cut ½-inch strips of dough from the long side of the rectangle. Fold the strips in half and with the palms of your hands roll the dough into breadsticks 10 inches long.

Arrange the breadsticks on nonstick baking sheets. Brush with the olive oil and sprinkle with the Hawaiian black lava sea salt.

Bake in the preheated oven for 10 minutes, turn the sticks over, and bake for another 10 minutes until golden. Leave to cool on a wire rack.

Italian-style flatbread
with puttanesca topping

1¾ cups all-purpose flour

1 teaspoon red chili flakes

1 teaspoon sel gris

⅔ cup warm water

2 tablespoons olive oil, plus extra for brushing

1½ teaspoons rapid-rise yeast (instant yeast)

¼ teaspoon brown sugar

¼ cup basil

¼ cup Italian parsley

olive oil, to drizzle

SERVES 4

Puttanesca topping

12 small cured black olives, pitted

1 cup cherry tomatoes

2 garlic cloves, finely chopped

1 tablespoon small salted capers

¼ small red onion, thinly sliced

1 teaspoon dried oregano

3 tablespoons olive oil

8 anchovy fillets

cracked black pepper and fleur de sel

To make the dough, mix the flour, chili flakes, and salt in a food processor. Pour the warm water into a measuring jug and add the olive oil, yeast, and brown sugar. Add the liquid to the flour mixture in a steady stream. Process until the liquid is incorporated and the dough forms a ball, about 3 minutes. Transfer the dough to a floured worktop and knead for about 3 minutes. Form into a ball and put in an oiled bowl. Cover and let prove in a warm place until it doubles.

To make the topping, put all of the ingredients in a bowl except the anchovies and seasoning and mix.

Preheat the oven to 475°F then roll the dough into a long oval and prick all over with a fork. Brush with olive oil, top with the puttanesca sauce and anchovies, then season. Bake the bread on a sheet for around 15 minutes until the dough is crisped. Sprinkle with the fresh herbs, salt, pepper and drizzle with olive oil.

Drinks and sweets

My Peach Margarita is best made in season when peaches are ripe and juicy, but you can also use frozen peaches. The chili salt adds a taste of Mexico. The mojito recipe is from my friend Manuel Rodriguez. He simply serves his citrus cocktail in pitchers, but I like to dust the rim of each glass with a pretty coating of lime salt. Salud!

Frozen peach margarita

¼ teaspoon chipotle chili powder
1 tablespoon Murray River salt flakes
¼ cup tequila
1 fl. oz. peach schnapps
1 large fresh peach, pitted and quartered, or 8 oz. frozen peaches

2 cups crushed ice
finely grated zest and freshly squeezed juice of 1 lime (reserve the squeezed fruits)

MAKES 1 LARGE SERVING

Mix together the chili powder and pink salt flakes. Wet the rim of a glass with the squeezed lime and dip into the chili salt. Set aside.

Put the remaining ingredients in a blender and blend until smooth. Serve in the salted glass.

Manny's mojito

1 cup fine white sugar
finely grated zest of 1 lime
4 tablespoons sea salt flakes
1 large bunch fresh mint, plus extra for garnishing
2 cups white rum

3 cups freshly squeezed lime juice, about 12 limes, (reserve the squeezed fruits)
2 cups soda water
crushed ice

SERVES 6

First make a simple syrup. Put the sugar and 1 cup water in a pan over medium heat. Simmer until all of the sugar has dissolved, then set aside to cool completely.

Mix the lime zest and sea salt, spread out on a small plate, and set aside.

Muddle the mint and rum in a large pitcher by mashing the mint against the side of the pitcher with the back of a wooden spoon. Leave for 30 minutes to let the flavors mingle.

Add the cooled syrup, lime juice, and soda water to the rum in the pitcher and stir. Add enough crushed ice to fill the pitcher. Garnish with mint sprigs.

Wet the rim of a tall glass with a squeezed lime, then dip the glass in the salt mixture and turn once. Do the same with the rest of the glasses then fill up with Manny's Mojito.

Dry-cured black olives make for a very hip martini. These Moroccan olives are picked ripe from the tree, washed and dried in the sun, then salted and packed in jars. Skewer them on a rosemary sprig for extra flavor and wow factor. Bloody Mary, a classic brunch drink, just gets better with a rim of celery salt. When making the celery salt, the leaves are dried in the oven on a wire rack so that warm air can circulate around the leaves.

Black olive martini

3 cured black olives, pitted
1 fresh rosemary sprig
1 teaspoon dry vermouth,
    such as Noilly Prat
¼ cup gin

ice

a cocktail shaker

SERVES 1

Skewer the olives on the rosemary sprig. Pour the vermouth into a chilled glass, swirl, and pour out. Fill a cocktail shaker with ice and pour in the gin. Shake and strain the gin into the glass.

Garnish with the olive skewer and serve immediately.

Bloody Mary *with celery salt*

1 small bunch celery, with
    leaves
1 tablespoon Jurassic salt
ice
5 cups chilled tomato or
    vegetable juice
1 cup chilled citron vodka
3 teaspoons
    Worcestershire sauce
2 teaspoons hot sauce or
    Tabasco sauce

1 tablespoon balsamic
    vinegar
finely grated zest and
    freshly squeezed juice
    of 1 lemon (reserve
    the squeezed fruits)
cracked green
    peppercorns

SERVES 4

Preheat the oven to its lowest setting. Pick the leaves from the celery, place on a wire rack, and put in the oven for 10–15 minutes until they are dried. Remove from the oven and let cool.

When ready to serve, put the dried celery leaves and Jurassic salt in a mini food processor or a salt grinder, grind, and empty onto a small plate. Wet the rims of 4 glasses with the reserved squeezed lemon and dip in the celery salt.

Fill a tall pitcher with ice and pour in the tomato juice, vodka, Worcestershire sauce, hot sauce, balsamic vinegar, and lemon zest and juice. Season liberally with cracked green peppercorns and a little of the celery salt. Stir and pour into the salted glasses. Garnish with a celery stick and serve.

You may think this combination sounds a little odd, but trust me this is a divine cookie. One bite and you will feel the explosion of tastes between the dark rich sweetness of the chocolate and fleur de sel salt. Use only the best fleur de sel from Guérande in France.

Chocolate sea salt cookies

1 cup all-purpose flour
½ cup cocoa powder
½ teaspoon baking powder
½ teaspoon baking soda
12 oz. bittersweet chocolate (70% cocoa solids), roughly chopped
¾ cup unsalted butter, room temperature
¾ cup dark brown sugar
¼ cup superfine sugar
1 egg
1 teaspoon pure vanilla extract
1 teaspoon rum
fleur de sel, to sprinkle

2 baking sheets, lined with parchment paper

MAKES APPROXIMATELY 24

Preheat the oven to 350°F.

Sift together the flour, cocoa powder, baking powder, and baking soda and set aside.

Melt 4 oz. bittersweet chocolate, either in a bowl over a saucepan of simmering water or in a microwave.

Cream together the butter and sugars in a food processor on high speed until light and fluffy, scraping down the sides of the bowl if necessary. Add the egg, vanilla extract, rum, and melted chocolate. Continue to beat for 2 minutes. Reduce the speed to slow and add the flour mixture. When that is well mixed, stir in the remaining chopped chocolate.

Put the mixture in the refrigerator for 5 minutes to harden slightly. Scoop tablespoons of the mixture onto the lined baking sheets, 2 inches apart (a small ice cream scoop is good for this). Flatten slightly with the back of the scoop. Sprinkle a little fleur de sel on top of each cookie and bake in the preheated oven for 10 minutes.

A spicy taste from south of the border, these salty chili chocolate truffles, rolled in Mexican Ibarra chocolate and Himalayan pink rock salt, are divine! You won't be able to stop eating them. Mexican Ibarra chocolate disks are made with chocolate mixed with cocoa beans and cinnamon. Buy them at Latin food markets.

Mexican chocolate chili-salted truffles

8 oz. bittersweet chocolate (70% cocoa solids), roughly chopped
¼ cup pouring cream
1 tablespoon unsalted butter
½ teaspoon confectioner's chili oil

Salted cocoa dusting powder
3 oz. Ibarra chocolate disks, roughly chopped
1 tablespoon Himalayan pink rock salt

a melon baller

MAKES 40

Put the chopped chocolate, cream, and butter in a heatproof bowl. Place the bowl over a pan of simmering water, making sure the water does not touch the bottom of the bowl. Once the chocolate has started to melt, stir gently until the mixture is smooth and creamy.

Stir in the chili oil and pour the mixture into a shallow bowl. Refrigerate until firm.

To make the dusting powder, process the Ibarra chocolate to a powder in a food processor. Pour it into a bowl and mix in the Himalayan salt.

When the chocolate mixture has set, scoop out the truffles with the melon baller and roll into balls. Toss in the dusting powder and serve.

Notes You can adjust the amount of chili oil to taste.

If you can't find Ibarra chocolate, you can make a similar dusting powder by mixing these ingredients: ⅓ cup white sugar, ⅓ cup cocoa powder, 1 teaspoon cinnamon, and 1 tablespoon Himalayan pink rock salt.

Brines, butters, dips, and rubs

Brines

Remember, once you have brined foods you must throw away the brine mixture; it cannot be used for anything else.

Beer brine for the barbecue

Brining ribs and chops really keeps them moist when they hit that fiery grill. You can leave meats in the brine for 2–3 days; the longer the better.

4 cups boiling water
1 bottle Guinness or dark beer
¼ cup coarse rock salt
3 tablespoons dark brown sugar
3 tablespoons molasses
1 tablespoon dried oregano

MAKES 6 CUPS

Put all the ingredients in a large bowl, stir until dissolved, and set aside. When the brine has cooled completely, it is ready to use.

Chile brine

This chile brine is excellent for shrimp in their shells. Only brine seafood for 20 minutes; after that the meat will begin to break up.

¼ cup sea salt
2 tablespoons dark brown sugar
6 dried red chiles
1 tablespoon coriander seeds
4 kaffir lime leaves

MAKES 6½ CUPS

Put all of the ingredients in a saucepan with 6 cups water and bring to a boil. Let simmer for 5 minutes. Set aside. When the brine has cooled completely, it is ready to use.

Sweet tea brine

Infusing chicken in this sweet tea brine gives the final dish a special taste. Fruity and light, it is the perfect brine for fried chicken.

4 tablespoons black tea leaves
6 cups boiling water
¼ cup coarse rock salt
3 tablespoons dark brown sugar
¼ cup honey

MAKES 7 CUPS

Put the black tea leaves in a measuring jug and pour over the boiling water. Add the salt, sugar, and honey and stir until dissolved. Set aside. When the brine has cooled completely, it is ready to use.

Pickled limes

Pickled limes are a great way to jazz up recipes. They're quick and easy to make and are ready in 1 month.

1 cup sea salt
12 limes, quartered
5 kaffir lime leaves
1 tablespoon pink peppercorns
freshly squeezed juice of 6 limes

a sterilized 1 quart jar*

MAKES 1 QUART

Put 1 tablespoon salt in the sterilized jar and layer with 4 lime quarters. Sprinkle with 2 tablespoons salt, then put 2 kaffir lime leaves and a few peppercorns on top. Continue to layer in this way, packing the limes down firmly as you go, until the jar is full. You may need to push the limes down.

Finish with a layer of salt and pour the lime juice over, to cover the limes. Seal the jar and store in a cool dark place for 1 month before using. Only use the skins of the limes; cut away and discard the pith and flesh.

*To sterilize, wash the jar in hot soapy water and rinse. Put the jar in a preheated oven at 350°F for 10 minutes.

From left: sweet tea brine, chili brine, pickled limes, and beer brine

Butters

To make the following butters, except the Salty Peanut Butter, put all the ingredients in a food processor and mix until smooth. Refrigerate until ready to use.

For ease of serving, make a butter roll by putting the butter mixture on a piece of plastic wrap. Fold the plastic wrap over the butter and roll it into a sausage shape. Twist the ends, refrigerate, and when cold and firm slice the butter into discs to use.

BUTTER RECIPES MAKE ½ CUP UNLESS INDICATED

Tuna butter

This is a variation of tonnato sauce. It's perfect to finish off a piece of grilled fish or chicken, and delicious just spread on a cracker.

1 stick unsalted butter
2 oz. canned tuna
finely grated zest and freshly
   squeezed juice of 1 small lemon
1 teaspoon Dijon mustard
1 tablespoon salted capers (do not
   rinse off the salt)
cracked black pepper, to taste

MAKES ¾ CUP

Anchovy butter

The sharpness of brined cornichons brings out the saltiness of the anchovies in this butter. Perfect for spreading on fresh wholemeal bread.

1 stick unsalted butter
4 salted anchovy fillets
1 oz. chopped cornichons
finely grated zest and freshly
   squeezed juice of 1 small lemon
cracked black pepper, to taste

Lemon caper butter

This simple butter goes perfectly with pan-fried fish.

1 stick unsalted butter
finely grated zest and freshly
   squeezed juice of 1 small lemon
1 tablespoon salted capers (do not
   rinse off the salt)

Green pepper butter

This is a really simple way of making a quick steak au poivre; just melt a dollop on a grilled steak and let the butter do the rest.

1 stick unsalted butter
2 tablespoons brined green
   peppercorns
sel gris and cracked black pepper,
   to taste

Indian butter

This butter is excellent spread on naan bread and warmed under the grill, or mix a tablespoon through basmati rice just before serving.

1 teaspoon each coriander seeds
   and cumin seeds, dry-roasted in a
   small sauté pan until light brown
1 stick unsalted butter
1 garlic clove, chopped
1 teaspoon smoked paprika
1 teaspoon chili powder
1 teaspoon curry powder
1 teaspoon sea salt
cracked black pepper, to taste

Salty peanut butter

Homemade peanut butter is so different from store-bought. If you can't find old-fashioned blistered peanuts, regular salted peanuts also work well.

1½ cups salted blistered peanuts
¼ cup peanut oil

MAKES 1 CUP

Put the peanuts in a food processor. With the motor running, pour in the peanut oil in a steady stream. Process until all the oil is incorporated and the nuts are evenly ground.

From top clockwise: lemon caper butter, tuna butter, Indian butter, salty peanut butter, green pepper butter, and anchovy butter.

Dips and rubs

Dips and rubs are easy to make, often from cupboard ingredients. They brighten up even the dullest slices of bread or cuts of meat.

Anchoïade

A flavorsome Provençal dip. Spread liberally on toasted baguette slices.

2 oz. canned anchovies in oil
3 garlic cloves, finely chopped
½ teaspoon herbes de Provence
finely grated zest and freshly
    squeezed juice of ½ lemon
1 oz. blanched almonds
2 tablespoons Italian parsley
2 tablespoons olive oil
½ teaspoon fleur de sel
cracked black pepper, to taste

SERVES 2

Put all the ingredients except the pepper in a food processor and process until a thick paste forms. Season with cracked black pepper.

Dukkah

A traditional Egyptian dip. You dip a piece of bread into olive oil and then into the dukkah. I also like to use it as a coating for meat and poultry.

¼ cup each hazelnuts, fennel seeds,
    cumin seeds, and coriander seeds
3 oz. sesame seeds
1 teaspoon sel gris
½ teaspoon cracked black pepper

MAKES 1¼ CUPS

In a hot pan, toast the hazelnuts and each of the spices separately. Let cool slightly then put all the ingredients in a food processor and pulse a few times.

Bagna cauda

Try dipping an assortment of grilled vegetables into this delicious sauce. Serve with crusty bread.

4 garlic cloves, roughly chopped
½ cup anchovy fillets in oil
finely grated zest of 1 lemon and
    freshly squeezed juice of ½ lemon
¼ cup olive oil
cracked black pepper and sea salt
    flakes, to taste

SERVES 2

In a food processor, mix the garlic and anchovies. Transfer to a small pan, add the lemon zest and juice, and warm over low heat. Gradually mix in the olive oil. Do not let the anchovies boil; they should be warmed through. Season to taste.

Muhammara

Serve this refreshing Middle Eastern dip with flatbreads.

1 cup walnuts
½ cup fresh brown bread crumbs
1 hot red chile pepper, such as
    Serrano, chopped
1 garlic clove, roughly chopped
3 tablespoons pomegranate molasses
½ teaspoon ground cumin
½ teaspoon ground coriander
½ teaspoon smoked paprika
¾ cup fresh pomegranate seeds
½ cup walnut oil, plus extra to drizzle
sea salt, to taste
a handful of mint leaves, to garnish

MAKES 2 CUPS

Toast the walnuts in a sauté pan for 2–3 minutes. Let cool, then put in a food processor with the other ingredients, reserving one-third of the pomegranate seeds. Process until slightly chunky. Season with sea salt. Put in a bowl and garnish with the remaining seeds, torn mint leaves, and a drizzle of walnut oil.

From top right clockwise: salted herbes de Provence, anchoïade, muhammara, harissa, bagna cauda, and dukkah.

Harissa

Harissa is a North African chili purée; use as a flavoring or a rub.

1 teaspoon cumin seeds
1 teaspoon coriander seeds
3 small red bell peppers, roasted until blistering, or store-bought
3 hot red chiles, such as Serrano, roughly chopped (including seeds)
1 garlic clove, roughly chopped
½ teaspoon Jurassic salt
¼ cup olive oil

MAKES 2 CUPS

In a small pan, toast the cumin and coriander seeds. Peel the peppers. Put everything in a food processor and process until smooth. Store in a glass jar with a tight-fitting lid.

Salted herbes de Provence

Makes a great rub for meat or fish.

2 tablespoons each dried thyme, dried rosemary, dried basil, fennel seeds, dried winter savory, and Murray River salt flakes
3 tablespoons dried lavender flowers

MAKES ¾ CUP

Mix all the ingredients in a bowl. Store in a glass jar.

SALT SOURCES

Surfas
8777 Washington Blvd
Culver City, CA 90232
(310) 558 1458
http://www.surfasonline.com

Saltworks
http://www.saltworks.us
1 800 353 7258

Salt Traders
http://www.salttraders.com
1 800 641 7258

The Meadow
1 888 388 4633
http://www.atthemeadow.com

ACKNOWLEDGMENTS

Thank you to Alison Starling for asking me to write about an ancient and fascinating ingredient in our daily life. It has been so much fun. Clare Double for expertly guiding me and Megan Smith's wonderful art direction. Jonathan Gregson's mouth-watering photography and great sense of humor. Huge thanks to Janis Voigt for running the kitchen and her marvelous cooking. My family and friends for cheering me on. Most of all thank you to my husband, who joyfully taste-tested everything with me.

CONVERSION CHART

Weights and measures have been rounded up or down slightly to make measuring easier.

Volume equivalents:

American	Metric	Imperial
6 tbsp butter	85 g	3 oz.
7 tbsp butter	100 g	3½ oz.
1 stick butter	115 g	4 oz.
1 teaspoon	5 ml	
1 tablespoon	15 ml	
¼ cup	60 ml	2 fl.oz.
⅓ cup	75 ml	2½ fl.oz.
½ cup	125 ml	4 fl.oz.
⅔ cup	150 ml	5 fl.oz. (¼ pint)
¾ cup	175 ml	6 fl.oz.
1 cup	250 ml	8 fl.oz.

Oven temperatures:

180°C	(350°F)	Gas 4
190°C	(375°F)	Gas 5
200°C	(400°F)	Gas 6
220°C	(425°F)	Gas 7
230°C	(450°F)	Gas 8
240°C	(475°F)	Gas 9

Weight equivalents:		Measurements:	
Imperial	Metric	Inches	Cm
1 oz.	30 g	¼ inch	0.5 cm
2 oz.	55 g	½ inch	1 cm
3 oz.	85 g	¾ inch	1.5 cm
3½ oz.	100 g	1 inch	2.5 cm
4 oz.	115 g	2 inches	5 cm
5 oz.	140 g	3 inches	7 cm
6 oz.	170 g	4 inches	10 cm
8 oz. (½ lb.)	225 g	5 inches	12 cm
9 oz.	250 g	6 inches	15 cm
10 oz.	280 g	7 inches	18 cm
11½ oz.	325 g	8 inches	20 cm
12 oz.	340 g	9 inches	23 cm
13 oz.	370 g	10 inches	25 cm
14 oz.	400 g	11 inches	28 cm
15 oz.	425 g	12 inches	30 cm
16 oz. (1 lb.)	450 g